KNOWING THE BIBLE

J. I. Packer, Theological Editor
Dane C. Ortlund, Series Editor
Lane T. Dennis, Executive Editor

• • • • • •

Genesis	Psalms	Jonah, Micah, and Nahum	Ephesians
Exodus	Proverbs		Philippians
Leviticus	Ecclesiastes	Haggai, Zechariah, and Malachi	Colossians and Philemon
Numbers	Song of Solomon		
Deuteronomy	Isaiah	Matthew	1–2 Thessalonians
Joshua	Jeremiah	Mark	1–2 Timothy and Titus
Judges	Lamentations, Habakkuk, and Zephaniah	Luke	
Ruth and Esther		John	Hebrews
1–2 Samuel	Ezekiel	Acts	James
1–2 Kings	Daniel	Romans	1–2 Peter and Jude
1–2 Chronicles	Hosea	1 Corinthians	1–3 John
Ezra and Nehemiah	Joel, Amos, and Obadiah	2 Corinthians	Revelation
Job		Galatians	

• • • • • •

J. I. PACKER is the former Board of Governors' Professor of Theology at Regent College (Vancouver, BC). Dr. Packer earned his DPhil at the University of Oxford. He is known and loved worldwide as the author of the best-selling book *Knowing God*, as well as many other titles on theology and the Christian life. He serves as the General Editor of the ESV Bible and as the Theological Editor for the ESV *Study Bible*.

LANE T. DENNIS is CEO of Crossway, a not-for-profit publishing ministry. Dr. Dennis earned his PhD from Northwestern University. He is Chair of the ESV Bible Translation Oversight Committee and Executive Editor of the ESV *Study Bible*.

DANE C. ORTLUND is Chief Publishing Officer and Bible Publisher at Crossway. He is a graduate of Covenant Theological Seminary (MDiv, ThM) and Wheaton College (BA, PhD). Dr. Ortlund has authored several books and scholarly articles in the areas of Bible, theology, and Christian living.

EZEKIEL

A 12-WEEK STUDY

Michael Lawrence

CROSSWAY®

WHEATON, ILLINOIS

Crossway is a publishing ministry of Good News Publishers.

VP		30	29	28	27	26	25	24	23	22	21	20
16	15	14	13	12	11	10	9	8	7	6	5	4	3	2

TABLE OF CONTENTS

KNOWING THE BIBLE, as the series title indicates, was created to help readers know and understand the meaning, the message, and the God of the Bible. Each volume in the series consists of 12 units that progressively take the reader through a clear, concise study of one or more books of the Bible. In this way, any given volume can fruitfully be used in a 12-week format either in group study, such as in a church-based context, or in individual study. Of course, these 12 studies could be completed in fewer or more than 12 weeks, as convenient, depending on the context in which they are used.

Each study unit gives an overview of the text at hand before digging into it with a series of questions for reflection or discussion. The unit then concludes by highlighting the gospel of grace in each passage ("Gospel Glimpses"), identifying whole-Bible themes that occur in the passage ("Whole-Bible Connections"), and pinpointing Christian doctrines that are affirmed in the passage ("Theological Soundings").

The final component to each unit is a section for reflecting on personal and practical implications from the passage at hand. The layout provides space for recording responses to the questions proposed, and we think readers need to do this to get the full benefit of the exercise. The series also includes definitions of key words. These definitions are indicated by a note number in the text and are found at the end of each chapter.

Lastly, to help understand the Bible in this deeper way, we urge readers to use the ESV Bible and the *ESV Study Bible*, which are available in various print and digital formats, including online editions at esv.org. The *Knowing the Bible* series is also available online.

May the Lord greatly bless your study as you seek to know him through knowing his Word.

J. I. Packer
Lane T. Dennis

WEEK 1: OVERVIEW

▲

Where is God? This is not a question we typically ask when life is going well. But when the bottom drops out from under us, when everything we take for granted is called into question, this is often the first question we ask. The answer we fear, the answer our circumstances might suggest, is that God has abandoned us and wants nothing to do with us. And our response might be angry protestations that God is not being fair, or denial that anything is wrong in the first place, or despair that things could ever be different. Perhaps we even vacillate between all three of these responses.

This is the situation facing Ezekiel and his fellow exiles in Babylon. Their world has been upended after they have been included in the first wave of deportees from Judah following Nebuchadnezzar's initial invasion of the land. At first they maintain hope, but then news arrives that Jerusalem has fallen and the temple has been burned to the ground. Has God abandoned his people for good? Can the dead bones of Israel ever live again (see Ezek. 37:3)?

Amid alternating anger, denial, and despair on the part of the exiles, God calls Ezekiel to speak his words, and *only his words*, to them. Otherwise the prophet remains mute for more than five years. Often he is also told to act out God's message in dramatic street theater, since the people are not inclined to listen. At first his message is an uncompromising and unrelenting pronouncement of judgment on Israel and vindication of God's justice. But once judgment falls, Ezekiel's message turns, just as relentlessly, into a message of hope for the restoration of God's people. Although the people's sin drove him from their midst as they broke their covenant[1] with him, God will not abandon his people. He will overcome all their enemies and their sin and lead them like a shepherd to safe pastures. Not only will he make a new covenant with them; he will also make *them* new, and so will dwell with them forever.

But the message of Ezekiel is not only for exiled Israelites. For all who have put their faith in God and his Messiah, Jesus Christ, the answer to the question, "Where is God?" is clear: Despite our circumstances, despite our sin, God is with his people. He always has been, and he always will be. (For further background, see the ESV Study Bible, pages 1495–1501; available online at esv.org.)

▶ Placing Ezekiel in the Larger Story

Like the other major prophets (Isaiah, Jeremiah, and Daniel), Ezekiel stands at a climactic moment in Israel's history as the covenant curses of Deuteronomy 28:15–68 are finally brought to bear. For centuries, God has patiently borne his people's treachery, idolatry, and sin, but his patience has finally come to an end. While Isaiah stood at the beginning of this period, and Daniel at the end, Ezekiel and Jeremiah prophesy at the white-hot center of Jerusalem's fall. Jeremiah is in Jerusalem, amid the crashing tumult, with all the confusion and passion we would expect. Already in exile in Babylon, Ezekiel hears and observes events from afar, like distant thunder. As a result, his prophecy is marked by waiting and reflection, long pauses followed by dramatic moments as events occurring months and even years earlier finally burst upon the consciousness of the exilic community.

In this context, Ezekiel serves not only as the prosecutor of God's covenant lawsuit, vindicating God's judgment against his own people; he serves also as pastor to the despairing exiled flock, providing them hope that judgment is not God's final word to them. If they will repent, God will again be their God and dwell with them, and they with him. Central to this hope is the pouring out of God's Spirit in a new covenant with a new temple and a renewed worship. This hope will wait centuries more for its fulfillment, but with the coming of Jesus Christ, God incarnate, it has begun. He is the true temple, and in his death and resurrection he has established a new covenant of peace. He is the source of living water, which is the Holy Spirit.[2] Even now he dwells with his people. While we still await the final fulfillment of Ezekiel's visions, because of the resurrection we can be confident that the day will arrive when the proclamation that "the dwelling place of God is with man" (Rev. 21:3) will come to full fruition.

Key Verse

"My dwelling place shall be with them, and I will be their God, and they shall be my people. Then the nations will know that I am the LORD who sanctifies Israel, when my sanctuary is in their midst forevermore." (Ezek. 37:27–28)

Date and Historical Background

Ezekiel is noteworthy for its precise dating. The book begins with the prophet's first vision, which can be dated to July 31, 593 BC. This was four years into the exile of King Jehoiachin, who had been deported to Babylon along with the leaders of Israel for his rebellion against Nebuchadnezzar (2 Kings 24:10–16). It also seems that this first vision comes in Ezekiel's thirtieth year, the year he would have begun his duty as priest. In exile, God calls him to an even higher ministry. The final vision comes 20 years later, on April 28, 573 BC. In the interim, Zedekiah, the puppet king installed by Nebuchadnezzar, rebels and precipitates the siege and fall of Jerusalem 18 months later to Babylon's army in 586 BC.

The book is essentially chronological in its arrangement, with some material (e.g., chs. 25–32) topically grouped. It is organized around the climactic event of Jerusalem's fall. Prior to that catastrophe, Ezekiel's message is one of unrelenting judgment, first for Israel and then for the nations. After word comes of Jerusalem's fall, Ezekiel's mouth is again opened and his message turns to hope of future restoration for God's people.

While dealing primarily with God's judgment against Israel and the nations and with the hope for restoration, the primary audience is the exilic community in Babylon. Ezekiel not only explains their exile but also seeks to turn them from false hopes (denial, claims of injustice, ethnic pride, and trusting in their heritage) to their only real hope, repentance toward God and faith in his promises. Such repentance and faith will be demonstrated in a longing for God's glory and a commitment to holiness.[3] In the end, their hope lies not with themselves but with God and his unwavering commitment to act for the "sake of my name" in order to vindicate his reputation and holiness.

Outline

   I. Inaugural Vision (1:1–3:27)

  II. Judgment on Jerusalem and Judah (4:1–24:27)

     A. A promise of judgment and hope (4:1–11:25)

     B. The case for judgment opened (12:1–16:63)

C. The case for judgment closed (17:1–24:27)

III. Oracles against Foreign Nations (25:1–32:32)

IV. Hope after the Fall of Jerusalem (33:1–39:29)

    A. The fall of Jerusalem (33:1–33)

    B. Hope for God's people (34:1–37:28)

    C. The last battle (38:1–39:29)

V. Vision of Restoration (40:1–48:35)

    A. The new temple (40:1–46:24)

    B. The new creation (47:1–48:35)

▶ As You Get Started

Do you have a sense at the outset of this study of any specific emphases of Ezekiel? Without using your Bible, do any particular passages from Ezekiel come to mind? Has this biblical book already been meaningful to your own walk with the Lord in any specific ways?

What is your current understanding of what Ezekiel contributes to Christian theology? That is, how does this book clarify your understanding of God, Jesus Christ, sin, salvation, the end times,[4] or other doctrines?

What aspects of the prophecy of Ezekiel have confused you? Are there any specific questions you hope to have answered through this study?

_____

_____

_____

_____

_____

_____

_____

_____

_____

As You Finish This Unit . . .

Take a few minutes to ask God to bless you with increased understanding and a transformed heart and life as you begin this study of Ezekiel.

Definitions

[1] **Covenant** – A binding agreement between two parties, typically involving a formal statement of their relationship, a list of stipulations and obligations for both parties, a list of witnesses to the agreement, and a list of curses for disobedience and blessings for faithfulness to the agreement. The OT is more properly understood as the old covenant, meaning the agreement established between God and his people prior to the coming of Jesus Christ and the establishment of the new covenant (the NT).

[2] **Holy Spirit** – One of the persons of the Trinity, and thus fully God. The Bible mentions several roles of the Holy Spirit, including convicting people of sin, bringing them to conversion, indwelling them, empowering them to live in righteousness and faithfulness, supporting them in times of trial, and enabling them to understand the Scriptures. The Holy Spirit inspired the writers of Scripture, guiding them to record the very words of God. The Holy Spirit was especially active in Jesus' life and ministry on earth (e.g., Luke 3:22).

[3] **Holiness** – A quality possessed by something or someone set apart for special use. When applied to God, this term refers to his utter perfection and complete transcendence over creation. God's people are called to imitate his holiness (Lev. 19:2), which means being set apart from sin and reserved for his purposes.

[4] **End times** – A time associated with events prophesied in Scripture to occur at the end of the world and the second coming of Christ—also known as the "last days." Because the early church expected the return of Christ at any time, the end times can refer to the period between Christ's ascension and his return.

WEEK 2: THE APPEARANCE OF THE LIKENESS OF THE GLORY OF THE LORD

Ezekiel 1:1–3:27

The Place of the Passage

After a brief biographical and historical note, Ezekiel begins with one of the most amazing depictions of the glory of God in the entire Bible. Full of strange and potentially confusing symbols, Ezekiel's first vision forms the foundation for his call and commission in chapters 2–3 as the Lord's prophet to the exiles in Babylon. But while the vision assures Ezekiel that God is still on his throne despite the exile,[1] it also raises the question, "What is God doing in Babylon?" Answering that question is what the first section of the book (chs. 1–11) is all about.

The Big Picture

Although God's people are in exile, God still reigns and still speaks to them through his prophet, if they have ears to hear.

Reflection and Discussion

Read through the complete passage for this study, Ezekiel 1–3. Then review the questions below concerning the opening section of Ezekiel and write your notes on them. (For further background, see the *ESV Study Bible*, pages 1502–1506; available online at esv.org.)

1. The Throne of the Lord Approaches (1:1–28)

As the book begins, Ezekiel is 30 years old, the age at which he would have been installed as a priest in the temple at Jerusalem (Num. 4:3). Instead, something even more significant occurs: he sees "visions of God" (Ezek. 1:1). Describe in your own words what he sees. Is this something an artist could draw? Why do you think Ezekiel repeatedly uses the terms "likeness," "appearance," and "as it were" to describe his vision?

In Ezekiel's vision, the four creatures not only fly but also are each stationed next to "a wheel within a wheel" (v. 16). Above their wings, they carry an "expanse" on which sits a throne. This is a vision of God's mobile chariot-throne that can go "straight forward" in any direction "without turning," directed by God's Spirit (v. 12). Why would an exile in Babylon need to know that God reigns from a mobile throne? How does such knowledge encourage Christians, who are "elect exiles" (1 Pet. 1:1)?

Ezekiel realizes that he has seen a vision of God, and yet he calls it "the appearance of the likeness of the glory of the LORD" (Ezek. 1:28). In other words, words fail him in his attempt to describe God. What aspects of God's glory do you see in this passage? Ezekiel lies prostrate on the ground in humility before the awesome holiness and majesty of God. Does your view of God produce the same response? What would need to change about your understanding of God to produce this kind of worship?

2. The Prophet Commissioned (2:1–3:15)

The last thing Ezekiel says in chapter 1 is that he "heard the voice of one speaking" (1:28). The culmination of the vision is not visual but aural. God's voice calls Ezekiel to prophetic ministry to a "rebellious house" (2:5). What, then, is the significance of Ezekiel's being commanded to eat a scroll with writing on both sides (2:8–3:3)?

The Lord draws a contrast between foreigners with difficult speech and the Israelites. The former would have listened to Ezekiel, but God knows that Israel will not listen (3:4–7). Why would God send a prophet to people he knows will not listen? What does this suggest about the purpose of Ezekiel's ministry?

It takes seven days of silence for Ezekiel to recover from this first vision. What accounts for the "bitterness in the heat of my spirit" that he experiences (3:14)?

3. The Duty of a Watchman (3:16–27)

The responsibilities of a watchman are common to several prophets (see Isa. 21:6–9; Hos. 9:8; Hab. 2:1). Watchmen were stationed on a city wall to warn of impending danger. What is the particular emphasis of Ezekiel's duty as watchman? How does that duty affect his life?

The initial vision is reprised in Ezekiel 3:22–27. How does God ensure that Ezekiel will be a faithful watchman, speaking only the words God gives him? What does this tell us about the importance of these words?

Read through the following three sections on *Gospel Glimpses*, *Whole-Bible Connections*, and *Theological Soundings*. Then take time to consider the *Personal Implications* these sections may have for you.

Gospel Glimpses

HE WHO WILL HEAR, LET HIM HEAR. Ezekiel is told to preach "whether they hear or refuse to hear" (2:7). Jesus will echo the final verse of chapter 3 by concluding many of his parables, "He who has ears, let him hear" (3:27; compare Matt. 13:9). Spiritual life comes by hearing God's Word. The message of life does not depend on us or our efforts. Nor does it come only to the worthy and the righteous. God speaks to sinners. His words of warning lead to repentance and life. The fact that he speaks, rather than leaving us alone in our sin, is grace. And if we will hear, we will "surely live" (Ezek. 3:21).

SON OF MAN. Ezekiel is called "son of man" (or "son of Adam") 93 times by God, marking him out as a creature in the face of the Creator. He is filled with the Spirit (2:2), who enables him to hear, obey, and speak God's Word. It is not surprising, then, that this title will be one of Jesus' favorite self-designations. As the last Adam, Jesus fully identifies with us in our humanity; but he is without sin, and so is qualified to be our substitute. Anointed[2] by the Holy Spirit, Jesus not only *speaks* God's Word to us, he *is* God's Word, displaying God's glory and bringing life to all who receive him.

Whole-Bible Connections

THEOPHANY. God is a spirit, and thus is invisible. When he appears in visible form, in what is called a *theophany*, we know that a major turning point in the history of redemption has come. Each of the redemptive covenants in the Old Testament is accompanied by a theophany (e.g., Genesis 15; Exodus 19; perhaps 2 Samuel 7), and in Ezekiel 1, the enactment of the covenant curses is accompanied by a theophany as well. God speaks to many, but he appears only to a few—that is, until Jesus, who is the "radiance of the glory of God and the exact imprint of his nature" (Heb. 1:3). With the establishment of the new covenant, God appears not in visions and symbols but in human flesh.

CHERUBIM. We often think of cherubim as small, pudgy boys with stubby wings. But the Bible portrays these angels as terrifying. They first appear in Genesis 3, wielding a flaming sword and guarding the entrance back to Eden. Their next appearance is in Exodus 25, guarding the ark of the covenant, the footstool of God's throne, in the Most Holy Place. Their appearance here in Ezekiel is meant to remind us of both of their functions, as throne-bearers and as guardians of God's holiness. Their presence portends judgment. It is only with the coming of Jesus that we finally see angels put down their swords and take up singing!

Theological Soundings

GLORY. The Hebrew word for "glory" is *kabod*, meaning heavy or weighty. When referring to God's physical manifestation, the term is usually associated with brightness and light. But God's glory, his significance, is manifested through more than light. It is the sum total of his perfections and attributes,[3] his transcendence, his sovereign majesty, his holiness, and his merciful love. And yet, God's glory is not an abstract idea. Paul tells us that we have been given "the light of the knowledge of the glory of God in the face of Jesus Christ" (2 Cor. 4:6).

THE GOD WHO SPEAKS. Throughout Scripture, what sets God apart from the idols is that he speaks. While idols attract the eye, they impart a false confidence to the worshiper. They are mute and can neither explain the past nor tell the future (see Isa. 41:21–29). Not only does the God of Scripture create and govern all things by his word (Gen. 1:3ff.; Ps. 33:6; Heb. 1:3; 11:3; 2 Pet. 3:5); his Word is the only means of salvation (Rom. 10:8–17) and the final standard of judgment (Rom. 3:19). God's Word brings clarity to our confusion and light to our darkness. Life and death hang in the balance of hearing and receiving God's Word.

Personal Implications

Take time to reflect on the implications of Ezekiel 1–3 for your own life today. Consider what you have learned that might lead you to praise God, repent of sin, and trust more deeply in his gracious promises. Write down your reflections under the three headings we have considered and on the passage as a whole.

1. Gospel Glimpses

2. Whole-Bible Connections

3. Theological Soundings

----

4. Ezekiel 1–3

As You Finish This Unit . . .

Take a moment now to ask for the Lord's blessing and help as you continue in this study of Ezekiel. And take a moment also to look back through this unit of study, to reflect on some key things that the Lord may be teaching you.

Definitions

[1] **The exile** – Several relocations of large groups of Israelites/Jews have occurred throughout history, but "the exile" typically refers to the Babylonian exile, that is, Nebuchadnezzar's relocation of residents of the southern kingdom of Judah to Babylon in 586 BC. (Residents of the northern kingdom of Israel had been resettled by Assyria in 722 BC.) After Babylon came under Persian rule, several waves of Jewish exiles returned and repopulated Judah.

[2] **Anoint** – In Scripture, to pour oil (usually olive oil) on someone or something to set the person or thing apart for a special purpose. Anointing was performed for the high priest, for tabernacle vessels, for kings, and for prophets. The Hebrew word *Messiah* and its Greek equivalent *Christ* both mean "anointed one."

[3] **Attributes of God** – The distinctive characteristics of God as he is described in the Bible. These include eternality, faithfulness, goodness, graciousness, holiness, immutability, infinitude, justice, love, mercy, omnipotence, omnipresence, omniscience, self-existence, self-sufficiency, sovereignty, and wisdom.

WEEK 3: A PROMISE OF JUDGMENT AND HOPE

Ezekiel 4:1–11:25

▲

The Place of the Passage

In Ezekiel 4–24, the prophet speaks an almost unrelenting message of impending judgment against Israel. This message begins in chapters 4–11 not only with verbal warnings but also with sign-acts dramatizing the fate awaiting Jerusalem and its people (chs. 4–5). Ezekiel's message is not, "Repent before it is too late," but rather, "It is too late; the end is here" (chs. 6–7). This study's section ends about a year later with another vision. Ezekiel is given a tour of the temple in Jerusalem, where he learns the reason the glory of the Lord has departed from Jerusalem and has come to Babylon (chs. 8–11). But the final word from God is not one of judgment. Rather it is one of hope, that after judgment there will be grace for a remnant of the nation.

The Big Picture

Because of Israel's unfaithfulness and idolatry, the Lord will judge his people. Yet because of his grace and faithfulness, the Lord will become their sanctuary.[1]

21

▶ Reflection and Discussion

Read through the complete passage for this study, Ezekiel 4–11. Then review the questions below concerning this section of Ezekiel and write your notes on them. (For further background, see the *ESV Study Bible*, pages 1506–1514; available online at esv.org.)

1. God against Jerusalem (4:1–5:17)

For over a year, God commands Ezekiel to enact the siege against Jerusalem like a boy playing with toy soldiers (4:1–3), and then to dramatize the experience of those inside the city (4:9–17), which was not fun and games at all. Finally, the prophet dramatizes the final fate of the inhabitants, as he burns, slices, and scatters the hairs of his head (5:1–4). Through all this the prophet is to remain mute, unless God gives him something to say. Why is "street theater" particularly appropriate for Ezekiel's audience? (see 3:7).

Repeatedly in his sign-acts, Ezekiel plays the parts of both God and the people. Representing God, he presses the siege with "arm bared" (4:7) and weighs the inhabitants of Jerusalem in the scale (5:1). As the people, he eats the rations of starvation (4:10–12). As Ezekiel represents God, what is the significance of the "iron griddle" (4:3)? As he plays the people, what is the significance of the "cords" (4:8)?

The sign-acts and their motivation are explained beginning in 5:5. God declares that he will "satisfy" his wrath and has "spoken in my jealousy" (5:13). How does 5:11 help us to make sense of wrath and jealousy in God, emotions that are usually inappropriate in us?

2. The End Has Come (6:1–7:27)

Chapter 6 announces the judgment of God against the mountains of Israel. What is occurring on the mountains that incurs God's wrath?

God declares that the people's altars and idols will be "broken" and defiled by their own dead bodies (6:5–6), bringing the curse of Leviticus 26:30 to bear. Then he declares that those who survive will remember how God was "broken" over their idolatry, using the same word. How does this help us to understand God's feelings about our sin?

In Ezekiel 7, the focus of judgment switches to the "land of Israel," and the background is no longer idolatry and the curses of Leviticus 26 but rather social injustice and the prophecy of Amos 8. Five times in this chapter God says he will punish or judge Israel "according to your ways." In light of Amos 8, what "ways" are particularly in view?

Chapters 6 and 7 of Ezekiel are punctuated by repeated variations of the statement, "You shall know that I am the LORD" (6:7; compare 6:10, 13, 14; 7:4, 9, 27), but that knowledge is not the result of repentance and faith. What brings them to this knowledge? How does such knowledge reveal the glory of the Lord?

----

3. The Glory of God Departs (8:1–11:25)

Just over a year after his first vision, Ezekiel has a second vision, one in which he is transported to the temple in Jerusalem. In chapter 8, what does he see taking place there? Are we to understand this literally or spiritually?

In response to Israel's idolatry, God does to his own house and city what he did to the high places[2] in chapter 6: he defiles it with dead bodies (9:7). But God also marks out and spares a remnant. What distinguishes the remnant marked on their foreheads from those to be slaughtered? Why is Ezekiel concerned that the remnant might not survive (9:8)?

In 9:3, "the glory of the God of Israel" moves from the Most Holy Place to the threshold of the temple. Then, in chapter 10, "the glory of the LORD" mounts the chariot-throne seen in chapter 1 and moves to the "east gate of the house of the LORD." Finally, in chapter 11, "the glory of the God of Israel" departs Jerusalem entirely, heading east, to the Mount of Olives. Why does God depart in stages? What does this reveal about God? How does this help us understand God's appearance in Babylon in chapter 1?

For the second time, Ezekiel asks if God will make a "full end of the remnant" (11:13; compare 9:8). In reply, God declares that the true sanctuary for God's people is not a building in Jerusalem but the Lord himself. Further, he promises to make his people fit to worship in that sanctuary. How will he do so? How has he already begun?

Read through the following three sections on *Gospel Glimpses*, *Whole-Bible Connections*, and *Theological Soundings*. Then take time to consider the *Personal Implications* these sections may have for you.

Gospel Glimpses

SIN-BEARER. Sin must be punished. This is part of what Ezekiel illustrates when he bears the punishment of Israel and Judah (4:4ff.). But there is no end to the punishment we deserve for our sin against an infinite, holy God. If we are to be saved, we need someone to bear our punishment for us. While Ezekiel does not bear Israel's punishment vicariously, Jesus has done so, and not just for Israel but for all who put their faith in him.

HEART OF FLESH. When God promises to gather the remnant back to himself (11:17–20), this is not a promise to give them a second chance. Rather, it is a promise to change them so that their hearts will no longer be hard to God's

Word but, instead, soft and yielding to it. This is what the New Testament calls regeneration (see John 3). When God's Spirit causes us to be born again,[3] he gives us a new nature that desires to obey him rather than to rebel. Although sin remains, the presence of these new desires to love and follow God provides us assurance that we belong to him.

Whole-Bible Connections

TEMPLE. The story of the Bible is the story of God's desire to live with his people, and the temple is central to that story. The garden of Eden was a garden-temple, but sin resulted in man's banishment from that place. The tabernacle, and later the temple, made provision for dealing with sin and accommodated God's presence among his people. But, as we saw, sin drove God out (Ezek. 8:6). In fact, the true temple was never a place or a building but was always God himself. When God declares that he is a sanctuary for the exiles (11:16), he is pointing forward to Jesus, the true temple (John 2:21).

COVENANT CURSES. In the Bible, covenants establish and confirm relationships and promise blessings for faithfulness and curses for unfaithfulness. God himself stands as witness to his covenants with man. It is a matter of justice, then, that the curses fall on the unfaithful. God could not simply ignore Israel's unfaithfulness and still be God (Ezek. 6:9; compare Lev. 26:14–33). This is why Jesus, the Messiah, had to be born under the law, so that he could rightly bear the curse of the covenant on behalf of covenant-breakers like Israel—and us.

Theological Soundings

THE WRATH OF GOD. God's wrath is not like our anger; his righteous wrath is one of his attributes and therefore one of his perfections. The wrath of God is his settled, judicial disposition against sin and evil. It flows out of his goodness, for he is unwilling to let evil and injustice go unanswered. God's wrath ultimately highlights his glory, for it demonstrates his commitment to holiness and righteousness. And it measures the depth of his love, for he determined to bear his own wrath fully in the person of his Son for the sake of his elect.

A REMNANT. The theology of the remnant, developed by the Old Testament prophets, is the theology of election.[4] Ezekiel's repeated question, "Will you make a full end of the remnant?" (9:8; 11:13) is not without reason. Left to our own efforts, none would be saved. But God, for no reason other than sheer mercy, has chosen to save some (see Rom. 9:16, 27–30). The reason he elects any is not for their sake but for the sake of his glory (Rom 9:23). Praise God that our salvation depends not on our initiative but on his commitment to his own glory.

> ## Personal Implications

Take time to reflect on the implications of Ezekiel 4–11 for your own life today. Consider what you have learned that might lead you to praise God, repent of sin, and trust more deeply in his gracious promises. Write down your reflections under the three headings we have considered and on the passage as a whole.

1. Gospel Glimpses

2. Whole-Bible Connections

3. Theological Soundings

4. Ezekiel 4–11

As You Finish This Unit . . .

Take a moment now to ask for the Lord's blessing and help as you continue in this study of Ezekiel. And take a moment also to look back through this unit of study, to reflect on some key things that the Lord may be teaching you.

Definitions

[1] **Sanctuary** – In the Bible, a place set aside as holy because of God's presence there. The inner sanctuary of the tabernacle (and later the temple) was called the Most Holy Place.

[2] **High places** – Height may or may not have been a feature of these public sites where offerings were made to God or to false gods. Worshiping the Lord at a high place was legitimate before the time of the temple (1 Kings 3:2, 4). Later, "high places," even those where the Lord was worshiped, were forbidden (2 Kings 23:15). Worship was to take place only at the temple (see Deut. 12:5–6; 1 Kings 9:3).

[3] **Born again** – A phrase used by Jesus in John 3 to describe how a person enters the kingdom of God. Natural birth is not sufficient. Instead, through the work of the Holy Spirit and the grace of God, a person must experience a second, spiritual birth, in which he or she becomes a new person in Christ.

[4] **Election** – In theology, God's sovereign choice of a people for redemption and eternal life. Also referred to as "predestination."

WEEK 4: THE CASE FOR JUDGMENT OPENED

Ezekiel 12:1–16:63

The Place of the Passage

Having announced the irreversible judgment of God against Jerusalem, Ezekiel now takes on the role of district attorney, prosecuting God's covenant lawsuit against Israel and answering the people's objections. Chapter 12 provides another sign-act, prophesying the coming exile and death of Zedekiah and all who remain with him in Jerusalem. In chapters 12–14, Ezekiel answers several objections: (1) his prophecies are of the distant future and might never be fulfilled; (2) other prophets are announcing "Peace"; and (3) the leaders of Israel are seeking the Lord, so surely he will answer. Ezekiel concludes this section with two parables, each illustrating that God's judgment is both certain and well deserved. And yet, for no other reason than God's faithfulness, there is also a note of hope at the end of chapter 16, one shaft of light in the unremitting darkness of chapters 12–24.

The Big Picture

God is faithful to his promise to judge Israel's sin, but despite Israel's unfaithfulness, he is faithful also to his covenant of love.

Reflection and Discussion

Read through the complete passage for this study, Ezekiel 12–16. Then review the questions below concerning this section of Ezekiel and write your notes on them. (For further background, see the *ESV Study Bible*, pages 1514–1522; available online at esv.org.)

1. Exile Is Coming (12:1–20)

Ezekiel is told once again to act out an element of the coming judgment, this time the experience of fleeing into exile. The focus is on the fate both of Zedekiah, the puppet king installed by Babylon in 597 BC (vv. 12–13), and of the people (vv. 14–20). What is the goal of this prophecy? What does it suggest the exiles were futilely hoping for?

2. False Hopes Demolished (12:21–14:23)

Ezekiel now addresses three false hopes, or defenses, that the exiles trust in. First, there is the hope that Ezekiel's prophecies are about the distant future and might never come to pass. This is the thrust of the proverb recounted in 12:22. What is the Lord's response? In light of 2 Kings 25 and the *ESV Study Bible* notes, was the Lord proved right? Do you live as if the fulfillment of God's promises are imminent?

The second false hope is that other prophets, both male and female, are prophesying "Peace" in the Lord's name and promising a strong defense for Israel

(Ezek. 13:10), even resorting to magic to deceive (13:18–19). How does God describe these people? What will the judgment be against these false prophets? How will God prove their prophecies false?

The third false hope is that the leaders of the exiles are inquiring of the Lord through Ezekiel (14:1–3). What is the problem with their inquiry? What does it mean that they have "taken their idols into their hearts" (see 14:4, 7)? How are we tempted to do the same?

How does the Lord answer these leaders? Why does he emphasize that "I the LORD will answer him myself" (14:7)? What are the two goals God has in answering the false inquirers?

Chapter 14 ends with the sobering warning that not even the prayers of the most righteous saints of the Old Testament could save Jerusalem in her unfaithfulness. And yet God promises to spare a few (vv. 22–23; compare 5:3). What sort of consolation will those survivors provide? How does this support the overall thrust of this section?

---

3. Judgment Deserved, Yet Hope Remains (15:1–16:63)

Ezekiel now relates two parables demonstrating that Israel's judgment is well deserved. Israel has long been described as God's vine (see Ps. 80:8ff.; Isa. 5:1ff.) What is it about the vine that makes its burning appropriate? What does this say about the inhabitants of Jerusalem (see Rom. 9:21–24)?

The second parable, one of the most famous in the whole Bible, describes the history of Israel in terms of a foundling that God rescues, nurtures, and eventually marries, raising her to the status of a beautiful queen (16:1–14). How does the queen repay her husband's generosity and love (see vv. 15–34)? Who are Israel's "lovers"? What does Israel's "whoredom" tell us about the nature of idolatry? What other forms does Israel's unfaithfulness take (see vv. 20–21, 23–29)?

In verses 35–58, God announces the judgment for Israel's crimes, comparing her crimes to that of her sisters, Samaria and Sodom, who were bywords for wickedness and unfaithfulness. In what ways could the judgment be described as "poetic justice," in which the judgment fits the crime perfectly? What is the role of shame in God's judgment? Is it deserved? Why?

The chapter ends on an unexpected note of hope, as God remembers the covenant Israel broke and determines to make a new covenant (vv. 59–63). Why does he do this? What is the role of Israel's shame now, and how does God redeem it for his glory?

Read through the following three sections on *Gospel Glimpses, Whole-Bible Connections*, and *Theological Soundings*. Then take time to consider the *Personal Implications* these sections may have for you.

Gospel Glimpses

REPENTANCE. Nearly every other religion tells us to work harder and be better, so that God will accept us. But not Christianity. Instead, the gospel calls us to repent. Repentance is not trying harder to clean up our lives so that God will love us. Repentance is literally a turning away from trusting in God-substitutes (idols), and turning to God in faith. This is what Ezekiel says to the elders[1] of Israel in 14:6, and it is what Jesus came to preach: repent and believe in the gospel (Mark 1:15).

GRACE. At the end of chapter 16, God acts in grace to promise a new covenant to his people. But as the context makes clear, God's gracious decision to save is not simply an unmerited gift, it is a "contra-merited" gift. An unmerited gift is what we get on Christmas or a birthday. A contra-merited gift, meanwhile, is what the adulterous, murderous, whoring wife receives when her marriage is restored and her children returned. This is the grace we receive in the gospel. Praise God for the shed blood of Christ that has secured such a glorious gift for us.

Whole-Bible Connections

VINE. When Jesus declares in John 15 that he is the vine and his disciples are the branches, he is using one of the main images of Israel from the Old Testament, identifying himself as the true Israel. In the Old Testament, the vine Israel is typically described as God's choice planting that has gone wild or become fruitless and useless. By identifying with his people, Jesus not only bears the punishment due such a useless vine (Ezekiel 15) but also, in his life, bears the fruit Israel should have borne, making all who are united with him by faith fruitful as well. To be cut off from Christ, though, is to remain in the state of being dead and useless, fit only for burning (John 15:4–6).

ADULTERY. It is common today for people to discount the Bible's sexual morality as outdated or invasive. But according to Paul's teaching in Ephesians 5:29–32, from the beginning God has designed marriage to reflect the pattern of Christ and his church. Marriage is a picture of the gospel, hardwired into creation. But this also means that adultery, and sexual immorality in general, is also a picture of something: idolatry. Ezekiel is not the only prophet to develop this theme, though he might be the most graphic. God hates adultery not only because of the harm it does to marriage but also because he hates idolatry, the spiritual adultery that physical adultery depicts.

Theological Soundings

ATONEMENT. God declares that he will establish his new covenant when "I atone for all that you have done" (Ezek. 16:63). Atonement[2] is the act by which two parties are reconciled. God does not state in Ezekiel 16 how such atonement will take place, but the rest of the Bible makes clear that without the shedding of blood there is no forgiveness[3] of sins (Heb. 9:22). In the Old Testament, worshipers made atonement by offering a sacrifice to God, usually through the priest. But here God declares that *he* will atone for his people's sin, which he accomplishes not through the blood of bulls and goats but through the blood of his own Son, Jesus Christ (Heb. 10:4–10).

Personal Implications

Take time to reflect on the implications of Ezekiel 12–16 for your own life today. Consider what you have learned that might lead you to praise God, repent of sin, and trust more deeply in his gracious promises. Write down your reflections under the three headings we have considered and on the passage as a whole.

1. Gospel Glimpses

2. Whole-Bible Connections

3. Theological Soundings

4. Ezekiel 12–16

As You Finish This Unit . . .

Take a moment now to ask for the Lord's blessing and help as you continue in this study of Ezekiel. And take a moment also to look back through this unit of study, to reflect on some key things that the Lord may be teaching you.

Definitions

[1] **Elder** – A recognized leader charged with oversight of a community or organized body. In the NT, an officer in the local church (Acts 14:23; 1 Tim. 3:1–7) charged primarily with spiritual oversight.

[2] **Atonement** – The reconciliation of a person with God, often associated with the offering of a sacrifice. Through his death and resurrection, Jesus Christ made atonement for the sins of believers. His death satisfied God's just wrath against sinful humanity, just as OT sacrifices symbolized death as payment for sin.

[3] **Forgiveness** – Release from guilt and the reestablishment of relationship. Forgiveness can be granted by God to human beings (Luke 24:47; 1 John 1:9) and by human beings to those who have wronged them (Matt. 18:21–22; Col. 3:13).

WEEK 5: THE CASE FOR JUDGMENT CLOSED

Ezekiel 17:1–24:27

The Place of the Passage

Ezekiel continues to prosecute God's covenant lawsuit against Israel. Chapters 17–20 address four additional self-deceptive defenses upon which Israel relies. By the end of chapter 20 God has settled his case, even though Israel still refuses to listen. Chapters 21–24 unfold the coming judgment prophetically with cinematic imagery. The sword is drawn in chapter 21, and as it is poised to strike, chapters 22–23 provide a flashback summary of why the judgment is deserved. Chapter 24 opens with a precise date, as God reveals that on that very day the final siege of Jerusalem has begun. The sword has struck. The section closes with heart-wrenching street theater, as God makes Ezekiel a sign to the exiles once again, this time through the unmourned death of his wife.

The Big Picture

Do not trust in man or anything man does for salvation, but trust in the Lord, for when the Lord saves, he saves for the sake of his name, not ours.

> ## Reflection and Discussion

Read through the complete passage for this study, Ezekiel 17–24. Then review the questions below concerning this section of Ezekiel and write your notes on them. (For further background, see the *ESV Study Bible*, pages 1522–1535; available online at esv.org.)

1. Case Closed (17:1–20:32)

Ezekiel addresses four self-deceptive defenses that the people of Israel rely upon to assure themselves that judgment will not happen. Chapter 17 addresses the political defense, that strong allies will save them, using a parable of two eagles and a vine. Whom do the eagles and the vine represent? Why does God say that the oath to Babylon that Zedekiah broke was actually broken against God (17:19)?

Chapter 18 addresses the ethical defense that claims that Israel does not deserve judgment. Who does Israel think is responsible, according to the proverb of sour grapes (v. 2)? How does God respond to this argument?

In light of their responsibility, God calls Israel to repentance. What is Israel's objection to repentance (v. 25)? What are they trying to protect by claiming that God is not fair? What happens when God judges us by the standard of our own self-assured righteousness? What does God's call to repentance reveal about him (see v. 32)?

The third defense, in chapter 19, rests upon national pride in the Davidic throne. Self-assurance in the might of princes is implied ironically, however, for the entire chapter is a lament for the princes of Israel. What sort of kings did the Davidic throne produce, and what happened to them, according to verses 1–9? Who are the two cubs?

The imagery shifts from lion cubs to a regal vine in the second half of the lament (vv. 10ff.). What is the fate of the vine? What are the intended effects of this lament on those who put their hope in the strength of the king in Jerusalem?

The final defense, in chapter 20, centers on Israel's special relationship with God, represented by the elders' inquiring of God through Ezekiel. But God instructs Ezekiel to turn Israel's history into a judgment against them (v. 4). What are some of the recurring themes about both God and Israel that Ezekiel's history highlights? Were there ever any "good old days," in Ezekiel's telling?

2. Salvation for My Name's Sake Alone (20:33–49)

The case against Israel ends with God's assurance that, though they want to be like the nations, God will never let that happen (20:32). What follows is the main passage of hope for this entire section. God declares that he will be their King (20:33), and though he judges them, he will also gather them and accept them (20:40). Why does God commit himself to them in this way? What does it mean for us that God ties his reputation to our salvation?

----

3. The Sword of the Lord (21:1–24:27)

God declares that he has drawn his sword of judgment against his people, and it will not be sheathed until it has accomplished its purpose (21:1–5). That sword is embodied by Nebuchadnezzar, but it is God who wields it. How does Ezekiel's sign-act of drawing a map and making a signpost make this point (21:18–23)?

Before the sword strikes, in two scenes that function almost like movie flash-backs, Ezekiel reviews the justness of the judgment about to fall. In chapter 22, Ezekiel is told by God to judge the "bloody city" (v. 2). Why is it bloody? What does its bloodiness signify before the Lord? How is this idea reinforced and developed in the image of dross, beginning in verse 17?

Chapter 23 allegorically[1] reviews Israel's unfaithfulness toward God as demonstrated in trusting in foreign powers and their gods. The two sisters represent the capitals of the northern and the southern kingdom, respectively. And, if anything, this portrayal is even more graphic than the one in chapter 16. While we do not talk this way in polite company, why does God use such explicit and graphic imagery to describe his people and their actions?

Ezekiel describes the shameless hypocrisy[2] of Israel's religion (23:36–42) and the people's exhaustion as, "worn out by adultery" (v. 43). While these images are shocking and sickening to us, do we recognize the hypocrisy of our own sin? Do we recognize sin as a cruel taskmaster who uses us and wears us out? How can we gain this perspective?

The drumbeat of judgment for Israel comes to an end in chapter 24, when the Lord tells Ezekiel that the siege of Jerusalem has begun. It will last 18 months, and then take additional weeks if not months for a messenger to bring news of it to Babylon. God describes Jerusalem under siege as a pot of stew. Look back at Ezekiel 11:1–12. Why is this image particularly apt? What in fact happens to the pot and the meat in it?

When Jerusalem falls under siege, in a heart-wrenching sign-act the Lord takes Ezekiel's wife in death and tells the 35-year-old widower that he may not mourn for her (24:15–18). What is this sign meant to convey to the exiles (vv. 19–24)? What does it say about Ezekiel that he obeys?

Read through the following three sections on *Gospel Glimpses, Whole-Bible Connections,* and *Theological Soundings.* Then take time to consider the *Personal Implications* these sections may have for you.

Gospel Glimpses

THE TRUE KING. Twice in the midst of these oracles[3] of judgment, God promises that a King will come who will not be like the faithless, wicked kings he is judging. In 17:22–24, God promises that he will plant a "sprig" that will grow up into a "noble cedar." And in 21:25–27, amid the prophecy against Zedekiah, God declares that there will not be another king "until he comes, the one to whom judgment belongs, and I will give [the crown] to him." In the midst of judgment, God's plan all along is to send a true and better king who will deliver his people. That King is Jesus.

Whole-Bible Connections

FOREIGN ALLIANCES. Repeatedly in these oracles of judgment, Israel is condemned for making and trusting in foreign alliances. This goes back to God's instructions to the Israelites in Deuteronomy to show no mercy to the nations they dispossessed, lest they be tempted to worship their gods. By the time of the prophets, this principle has been extended to foreign alliances. As Isaiah declares, "Woe to those who go down to Egypt for help . . . but do not look to the Holy One of Israel" (Isa. 31:1). In the new covenant, this principle remains, but the focus is not on political alliances but rather on worldly means pursued for spiritual ends (see 1 Cor. 2:4–5).

Theological Soundings

READING PROVIDENCE. It is tempting to read providence, as Ezekiel was enabled to do in chapter 21. God is in control of history, and though events may seem to happen by chance, God is directing everything to the end that he has determined. But while we know that God is in control, and while we know how the story of history will end, unless God reveals the meaning of any specific event, we are cautioned against drawing direct cause-and-effect conclusions. Unlike Ezekiel, we are not prophets. At best, as John Flavel said, "The providence of God is like Hebrew words—it can be read only backwards." And so Deuteronomy 29:29 is our guide: "The secret things belong to the LORD our God, but the things that are revealed belong to us and to our children forever, that we may do all the words of this law."

Personal Implications

Take time to reflect on the implications of Ezekiel 17–24 for your own life today. Consider what you have learned that might lead you to praise God, repent of sin, and trust more deeply in his gracious promises. Write down your reflections under the three headings we have considered and on the passage as a whole.

1. Gospel Glimpses

2. Whole-Bible Connections

3. Theological Soundings

4. Ezekiel 17–24

As You Finish This Unit . . .

Take a moment now to ask for the Lord's blessing and help as you continue in this study of Ezekiel. And take a moment also to look back through this unit of study, to reflect on some key things that the Lord may be teaching you.

Definitions

[1] **Allegory** – A story that communicates truth through a symbolic understanding of its literal meaning. In allegory, characters, objects, and actions specifically represent things from the parallel spiritual or moral context. An example (in addition to Ezekiel 23) is in Galatians 4, where Paul interpreted the true story of Hagar (Genesis 16–21) as an allegory to make a point about how the Sinai covenant differs from the new covenant in Christ.

[2] **Hypocrisy** – Falsely presenting oneself to others in order to gain positive regard or praise. Derived from the Greek for "actor." Jesus repeatedly condemned the hypocrisy of Jewish religious leaders.

[3] **Oracle** – From Latin "to speak." In the Bible, it refers to a divine pronouncement delivered through a human agent.

Week 6: Judgment against the Nations

Ezekiel 25:1–32:32

The Place of the Passage

Ezekiel is told at the end of chapter 24 that a fugitive from Jerusalem is coming to announce that the city has fallen. But it will take weeks, if not months, for him to arrive. Into the midst of their anxious waiting, God declares his judgment on seven nations and their gods. This second major section of the book is carefully structured, both geographically and stylistically. The fulcrum of the passage is a brief statement of restoration for Israel (28:24–26). Thus this section serves not only to demonstrate that God is sovereign over the nations but also to offer backhanded hope to God's people. The judgment of their enemies implies the security of Israel's future. The drumbeat of judgment has begun to give way to the hope for salvation.

The Big Picture

God will ultimately deliver his people by defeating their enemies so that the whole world will know that the Lord is God.

> ### Reflection and Discussion

Read through the complete passage for this study, Ezekiel 25–32. Then review the questions below concerning this section of Ezekiel and write your notes on them. (For further background, see the *ESV Study Bible*, pages 1536–1552; available online at esv.org.)

Chapters 25–32 exhibit multiple layers of structure. Seven nations are addressed in a 6 + 1 arrangement, with a brief statement of hope coming before the final nation. The first six nations are addressed by moving around the points of the compass clockwise, beginning in the east. The longest oracles, those against the fifth (Tyre) and seventh (Egypt) nations, are each composed of seven internal sections. The length of the oracle against Egypt is equal to the length of the other six combined. All of this contributes to the message that God is not a local deity but is Lord over the entire world; he directs the affairs of nations and will hold them to account.

1. God Will Judge the Nations . . . (25:1–28:10, 20–23; 29:1–32:32)

In chapter 25, the first four nations judged (Ammon, Moab, Edom, Philistia) are Israel's closest neighbors. What is the common complaint that God has against each of them (see vv. 3, 8, 12, 15)? Why would this particularly invite God's wrath (see Deut. 32:41; Rom. 12:19)?

Chapters 26–28 of Ezekiel are directed against Tyre and her sister city, Sidon. Using the text and the *ESV Study Bible* notes, identify God's complaint against this city-state. Why does Tyre receive such inordinate treatment, compared to Israel's other near neighbors? Wealth, success, and pride go hand-in-hand. In what ways do you see wealth or success tempting you to trust in yourself?

Egypt was not only Israel's historical enslaver but also her recurring temptation to seek help apart from the Lord. It was Egypt that encouraged Zedekiah's rebellion against Babylon, which led to the current catastrophe. Once again using the text and the ESV *Study Bible* notes, identify God's complaint against Egypt. How does this parallel the charges against the other nations? How does the conclusion of the oracle (32:17–32) serve as a fitting answer to the pride of Egypt and the rest of the nations?

2. . . . and Their Gods (29:1–21; 30:13–19)

In the ancient Near East, battles between nations were considered battles between their gods. The victorious nation would believe it had won because its god was victorious. How does God's statement that Nebuchadnezzar "worked for me" subvert this idea (29:20)? What does God's description of Pharaoh as "the great dragon" seem to imply about who is being defeated (29:1–5)? Why do the exiles need to know that *spiritual* battles are being fought behind the military ones?

3. God Will Judge the Prince of Evil (28:1–19)

Chapter 28 contains two laments, one over the prince of Tyre (v. 1) and one over the king of Tyre (v. 11). While the same person is clearly in view, the language of the second lament moves beyond the natural to the supernatural, much as the language about Pharaoh does in 29:1–5. It is as if, flickering behind the face of Tyre's ruler, stands another prince, animating the rebellion of all the rest (compare Isa. 14:12–21). What about this language suggests that a supernatural figure is being addressed? Why is he condemned (Ezek. 28:15–18)? Why would this oracle be important in order to complete the encouragement of Israel?

4. God Will Gather His People (28:24–26)

At the center of this section stands a brief promise that God will gather his people securely. When will this gathering happen (v. 26)? At that time, God declares, there will no longer be "brier to prick or a thorn to hurt" (v. 24). To what does this image allude (see Gen. 3:18)? Given the context of the whole-world judgment implied by the seven nations' oracles, and the immediate context of what appears to be a judgment of Satan, what does this suggest about the ultimate horizon of fulfillment for this promise?

Read through the following three sections on *Gospel Glimpses, Whole-Bible Connections*, and *Theological Soundings*. Then take time to consider the *Personal Implications* these sections may have for you.

Gospel Glimpses

THE DRAGON DEFEATED. The good news of the gospel is not simply that our sins are forgiven. It also declares that Satan has been defeated. From the beginning, his goal has been the destruction of God's people, but in the crucifixion[1] and resurrection of Jesus Christ he has been defeated (Rev. 12:7–11). Although he still has the power to tempt and discourage until Christ returns, Satan's greatest weapon against the saints has already been broken, for every one of his accusations has been answered in the blood of Christ.

Whole-Bible Connections

GOD AS WARRIOR. Throughout Scripture, God is portrayed as the divine warrior who fights for his people in order to deliver them. It was God who brought the battle to the Egyptians and their gods in the plagues (Ex. 6:1ff.), and it was God who went before the armies of Joshua to fight for them (Deut. 1:30). At the start of Ezekiel, God rides into Babylon on a war chariot. But God's ultimate champion is Jesus, who did battle with Satan[2] at Calvary. There Jesus not only disarmed him but also made a spectacle of him, triumphing over him by the cross (Col. 2:15).

SPIRITUAL WARFARE. Throughout its history, Israel's enemies were the nations surrounding her, and the battles they fought were against flesh and blood. But with the coming of the Messiah and the new covenant, the battle has shifted. God's people, drawn now from every nation, are still beset with enemies, but those hostile forces are no longer flesh and blood but "spiritual forces of evil in the heavenly places." As such, our weapons in the fight are no longer political and military but are the spiritual weapons given to us in the "armor of God" (Eph. 6:12ff.).

Theological Soundings

UNIVERSALISM. Will everyone in the world be saved when Jesus returns? "Then they will know that I am the LORD" is repeated 18 times in these eight chapters. Most of these references have to do with the nations that God is judging. While it is true that, on the last day, knowledge of the Lord will be universal, it is not the case that all such knowledge will lead to salvation. There is a difference between knowing the Lord as judge and knowing the Lord as the one who took that judgment on your behalf. The former knowing leads only to a "fearful expectation" (Heb. 10:27), while the latter leads to "great joy" (Jude 24–25).

Personal Implications

Take time to reflect on the implications of Ezekiel 25–32 for your own life today. Consider what you have learned that might lead you to praise God, repent of sin, and trust more deeply in his gracious promises. Write down your reflections under the three headings we have considered and on the passage as a whole.

1. Gospel Glimpses

2. Whole-Bible Connections

3. Theological Soundings

4. Ezekiel 25–32

> ## As You Finish This Unit . . .

Take a moment now to ask for the Lord's blessing and help as you continue in this study of Ezekiel. And take a moment also to look back through this unit of study, to reflect on some key things that the Lord may be teaching you.

Definitions

[1] **Crucifixion** – A means of execution in which the person was fastened, by ropes or nails, to a crossbeam that was then raised and attached to a vertical beam, forming a cross (the root meaning of "crucifixion"). The process was designed to maximize pain and humiliation and to serve as a deterrent for other potential offenders. Jesus suffered this form of execution (Matt. 27:32–56), not for any offense he had committed (Heb. 4:15) but as the atoning sacrifice for all who would believe in him (John 3:16).

[2] **Satan** – A spiritual being whose name means "accuser." As the leader of all the demonic forces, Satan opposed God's rule and seeks to harm God's people and accuse them of wrongdoing. His power, however, is confined to the bounds that God has set for him, and one day he will be destroyed along with all of his demons (Matt. 25:41; Rev. 20:10).

WEEK 7: JERUSALEM HAS FALLEN

Ezekiel 33:1–33

The Place of the Passage

If the tone of the book began to change from judgment to hope after the announcement of the siege of Jerusalem in chapter 24, that pivot is complete by the time of the fall of the city in chapter 33. Ezekiel's role as watchman is reprised, but after these final words of judgment, the prevailing tone of the book becomes hopeful. Since the beginning, Ezekiel has been mute, speaking only when the Lord opens his mouth. With the arrival of a fugitive announcing the fall of Jerusalem, Ezekiel's mouth is opened, signifying a new disposition of the Lord toward his people.

The Big Picture

In the face of God's judgment, his people should neither trust in their own righteousness nor despair in their sin, but rather heed God's word and repent.

> **Reflection and Discussion**

Read through the complete passage for this study, Ezekiel 33. Then review the questions below concerning this section of Ezekiel and write your notes on them. (For further background, see the *ESV Study Bible*, pages 1552–1554; available online at esv.org.)

1. The Watchman Reprised (33:1–20)

Much of this section, composed of a reiteration of Ezekiel's responsibility as a watchman (vv. 1–9) and the people's responsibility to heed his warning and repent (vv. 10–20), repeats and parallels earlier material from 3:16–21 and 18:19–32. What might be the purpose for this reprise after the section outlining the judgment of the nations? Is there any indication that the response might be different this time?

The call to personal responsibility in verses 10–20 starts and ends differently than does the parallel in 18:19–32. The earlier passage started with an objection concerning God's justice and ended with a call to repentance and the command to "make yourselves a new heart and a new spirit" (18:31). This passage begins with the despairing question, "How then can we live?" (v. 10) and ends without the command being repeated. What might account for this change (see Ezek. 36:22–32; 37:1–28)? What does the fact that God does for us what we cannot do for ourselves teach us about him? How does this reinforce the message of 33:11?

2. The Fall of Jerusalem (33:21–22)

Two years after the siege began (see 24:1), and five or six months after the city fell, a fugitive arrives with news of Jerusalem's demise. How has the structure of Ezekiel reinforced the sense of waiting and impending doom the exiles must have felt between the announcement of the siege and the announcement of its success?

God had promised Ezekiel that on the day the fugitive arrived, Ezekiel's mouth would be opened and he would no longer be mute (see 24:25–27). How has Ezekiel been a sign to the exiles in his muteness? What does this suggest about the kind of sign he will be in his speech now?

3. A Warning for the Survivors (33:23–33)

Ezekiel warns both those left in the land and the exiles. What is his warning to those left in Israel? What are they trusting in? Why is their trust misplaced? What is the danger in trusting in our heritage or current status?

By contrast, what is the misplaced trust of the exiles (see vv. 31–32)? What is the danger in treating God's Word as entertainment and his spokesmen as celebrities? What does James say about the fate of one who is a "hearer of the word and not a doer" (see James 1:22–27)? How are we tempted to turn God's Word into entertainment to be enjoyed rather than words to be obeyed?

Read through the following three sections on *Gospel Glimpses, Whole-Bible Connections*, and *Theological Soundings*. Then take time to consider the *Personal Implications* these sections may have for you.

Gospel Glimpses

GOD'S COMPASSIONATE HEART. "As I live, declares the Lord GOD, I have no pleasure in the death of the wicked" (33:11). Contrary to the common misconception that God delights in zapping sinners with his thunderbolts, judgment is his "alien work," as the Puritans used to put it. His "native" work is salvation. And so, his call to repentance is not that of a cosmic killjoy who wants to spoil our fun but rather the call of a loving Creator who desires to see his creatures live. In our evangelism,[1] we should sound not only the note of warning but also the glorious message of a Creator whose heart longs for those created in his image.

Whole-Bible Connections

ABRAHAM'S DESCENDANTS. Misplaced hope in Abrahamic descent is a recurring theme in Scripture. This is the same mistake for which John the Baptist condemns the crowds and the Pharisees (Luke 3:7–9), and it is the temptation that trips up Peter (Gal. 2:11–14) and threatens to divide the Ephesian church (Eph. 3:6). But, as Paul reminds us, our hope is based not on our physical descent, nor on any other gift or attribute we may possess, but rather on our inclusion in Christ by grace through faith (Rom. 4:9–12; 5:1–2).

Theological Soundings

GOD'S JUSTICE. On multiple occasions in Ezekiel, God's people question God's justice (see 18:25–29; 33:17–20). What they are offended by is the fact that past good deeds do not make up for current evil deeds. But unlike human justice, which is necessarily relative, God's justice is absolute. Every righteous act we perform is one we already owed him. There are no acts of supererogation.[2] And therefore our good deeds, even if we could do them perfectly, could never make up for our sinful deeds. As James declares, "whoever keeps the whole law but fails in one point has become guilty of all of it" (James 2:10; compare Luke 17:10). Let us therefore thank God for his Son, Jesus Christ, who grants the merit of his good deeds to us, while on the cross receiving the guilt for all our sins, for which we could never atone.

Personal Implications

Take time to reflect on the implications of Ezekiel 33 for your own life today. Consider what you have learned that might lead you to praise God, repent of sin, and trust more deeply in his gracious promises. Write down your reflections under the three headings we have considered and on the passage as a whole.

1. Gospel Glimpses

2. Whole-Bible Connections

3. Theological Soundings

4. Ezekiel 33

> ### As You Finish This Unit . . .

Take a moment now to ask for the Lord's blessing and help as you continue in this study of Ezekiel. And take a moment also to look back through this unit of study, to reflect on some key things that the Lord may be teaching you.

Definitions

[1] **Evangelism** – Proclamation of the gospel (Greek *euangelion*) of Jesus Christ.

[2] **Supererogation** – Good works that go above and beyond that which is required.

WEEK 8: HOPE FOR GOD'S PEOPLE

Ezekiel 34:1–37:28

▲

The intimation from chapter 33 that God is going to act on behalf of his people now comes into full view. Condemning the faithless shepherds of Israel, God declares that he himself will be their Shepherd and will bring them into a place of prosperity and security in a covenant of peace (ch. 34). Condemning Edom and its wrongful grab for Israel's inheritance (ch. 35), the Lord promises that the mountains of Israel will burst into life and God will put his Spirit in his people, who will live with God as if in a new garden of Eden (ch. 36). This great reversal of fortunes is illustrated as God brings life to the valley of dry bones. Israel's future is not death but life under their Davidic shepherd-king, in a covenant of peace with their God who dwells in their midst (ch. 37).

The Big Picture

For the sake of his name, God will restore his people under the faithful rule of the Messiah by cleansing them from their impurity and putting his Spirit within them.

> ### Reflection and Discussion

Read through the complete passage for this study, Ezekiel 34–37. Then review the questions below concerning this section of Ezekiel and write your notes on them. (For further background, see the *ESV Study Bible*, pages 1554–1560; available online at esv.org.)

1. The Good Shepherd and His Sheep (34:1–31)

Who are the shepherds of Israel? Why does God condemn them (vv. 1–10)? What does their condemnation tell us about the role of shepherd-leaders in the community of God's people? In the New Testament, elders are to shepherd the church (see Acts 20:28). Can we learn anything from this passage about what sort of men they should be?

What does it mean when God says that "I myself will be the shepherd of my sheep" (v. 15)? What does God say he will do for the flock (vv. 11–16)? How will he do this (vv. 17–24)? Who is the shepherd-king that God will "set up over them" (v. 23)?

The language of verses 25–31 recalls the covenant blessings enumerated in Leviticus 26:1–13. But the old covenant also enumerated covenant curses. Why are the curses not mentioned in relation to the new covenant of peace that God will establish through the messianic King?

2. The Desolation of Edom and the Restoration of Israel (35:1–36:38)

Why is Edom condemned (35:5, 10, 12–13)? What will its punishment be (35:6–9, 14–15)? How does this contrast with the future of Israel (see 36:8–15)? How is this an example of poetic or ironic justice? What is the purpose of such justice?

What justification does God give for his judgment of the nations (36:2–7)? What does it mean to you that God is jealous over his people? What encouragement and hope should we find in this aspect of God's character?

In 36:16–20, God explains that he judged Israel "for their deeds." But in 36:21–38, God declares that he will save and restore Israel out of "concern for my holy name." How had Israel "profaned" God's name in exile? And what is required, therefore, for God to "vindicate"[1] his holiness in their salvation (36:24–32)? How will he accomplish the required internal cleansing?

The language of new hearts in a land echoing the garden of Eden (36:35) recalls Moses' promise that when God restored Israel from its exile, he would "circumcise your hearts" (Deut. 30:6). What is the effect of such new hearts? What does this say about the nature of the restored community? What effect will such a community have on the surrounding nations (Ezek. 36:36)? Is this the effect of your local church in your community? Why or why not?

----

3. The Valley of Dry Bones (37:1–28)

While the promise of chapter 36 is wonderful, God himself asks the question that must have been on Ezekiel's and his listeners' minds: "Can these bones [i.e., dead Israel] live?" (37:3). In other words, could this promised restoration actually happen? In response, God gives Ezekiel his third major vision (37:1–10). How does this vision answer the despair of the exiles (37:11–14)?

If we were writing this vision, we would probably have God put flesh on the bones before telling Ezekiel to speak to them. After all, how can someone hear without ears? But what is the point of Ezekiel's prophesying to desiccated bones? How does this recall the creation narrative of Genesis 1–2 (see Gen. 2:7)? How does it look forward to resurrection? Why must salvation be an act of re-creation, rather than merely reformation?

How does God create and re-create? What does this say about the role of preaching and God's Word today?

Ezekiel 37 ends with a promise of Israel's restoration as a single nation, living under David's rule, with God dwelling in their midst in his sanctuary (37:15–28). At this point, the northern kingdom has been in exile for 150 years, the line of David is broken, and the people have just learned that the temple had been razed. How might the exiles have felt about the promise of a restored nation and sanctuary? How do you respond to God's promises that feel impossible? Has God given us a "valley of dry bones" out of which we can take hope for God's seemingly impossible promises made to us?

Read through the following three sections on *Gospel Glimpses*, *Whole-Bible Connections*, and *Theological Soundings*. Then take time to consider the *Personal Implications* these sections may have for you.

Gospel Glimpses

GOOD SHEPHERD. The language related to a shepherd is kingly language in the Old Testament. David, for example, was the shepherd-king *par excellence*, following in the footsteps of the great Shepherd-King, the Lord himself (see Psalm 23; Ezek. 34:15). Shortly after declaring himself to be Israel's Shepherd, the Lord in Ezekiel 34:23 declares that David is the ultimate shepherd of his people. So, is the shepherd-king human or divine? When Jesus declares that he is the Good Shepherd (John 10), we have the answer. He is both the Davidic Messiah and the incarnate[2] God. And he is exactly the Shepherd-King that we need.

NEW HEART AND NEW SPIRIT. The good news of the gospel is that we are not only forgiven but also changed. If God simply forgave us and gave us a second chance, we would rebel against him again. Instead, through his Holy Spirit, God changes our very nature (Ezek. 36:26). He re-creates us, giving us a new heart and a new spirit that now desire to obey and follow him in faith (see Romans 8). And that heart will one day be perfected in glory. His goal is not simply our forgiveness but also our holiness.

Whole-Bible Connections

EDOM. The people of Edom are the descendants of Esau (Gen. 36:19), who despised his birthright and lost his inheritance (Gen. 25:29–34). Though Jacob and Esau are eventually reconciled, their enmity continues to play out in the Old Testament, culminating in Edom's land grab and the condemnation of the nation in Ezekiel and Obadiah. In the New Testament, Esau becomes a picture of all who turn away from the faith because of sinful unbelief or immorality (Heb. 12:16), demonstrating that they were never saved in the first place (Rom. 9:13).

HEART OF FLESH. From the beginning of the story of God's people, the need for changed hearts has been evident. Moses knew that Israel would break the covenant God had made with them, because though their flesh had been circumcised, their hearts had not been. Instead of being soft toward God, their hearts were hard (Deut. 10:16; 30:6). Jeremiah renewed the call for circumcised hearts (Jer. 4:4). But it would be Jesus who accomplished this change in his people, as he gave the gift of the Spirit promised in Ezekiel 36:27 (see John 3:34).

Theological Soundings

REGENERATION. "New heart" and "new spirit," "circumcision of the heart," and "heart of flesh" are different Old Testament images for regeneration. To be regenerated is to be "born again," to use Jesus' language from John 3. It is to be created anew. Regeneration is the sovereign and sole work of the Holy Spirit and is the necessary precondition for repentance and faith, from which flow all of the other blessings of salvation, such as adoption,[3] justification,[4] sanctification,[5] and glorification.[6] Unless God takes the initiative to give us new hearts, we simply cannot be saved.

Personal Implications

Take time to reflect on the implications of Ezekiel 34–37 for your own life today. Consider what you have learned that might lead you to praise God, repent of sin, and trust more deeply in his gracious promises. Write down your reflections under the three headings we have considered and on the passage as a whole.

1. Gospel Glimpses

2. Whole-Bible Connections

3. Theological Soundings

4. Ezekiel 34–37

As You Finish This Unit . . .

Take a moment now to ask for the Lord's blessing and help as you continue in this study of Ezekiel. And take a moment also to look back through this unit of study, to reflect on some key things that the Lord may be teaching you.

Definitions

[1] **Vindication** – Being cleared of accusation or blame.

[2] **Incarnation** – Literally "(becoming) in flesh," this term refers to God's becoming a human being in the person of Jesus of Nazareth.

[3] **Adoption** – The legal process by which a person gives the status of son or daughter to another person who is not his or her child by birth. The NT uses the term to describe the act by which God makes believers his children through the atoning death and resurrection of his one and only true Son, Jesus (see Romans 8; Galatians 4).

[4] **Justification** – The act of God's grace in bringing sinners into a new covenant relationship with himself and counting them as righteous before him through the forgiveness of sins (Rom. 3:20–26).

[5] **Sanctification** – The process of being conformed to the image of Jesus Christ through the work of the Holy Spirit. This process begins immediately after regeneration and continues throughout a Christian's life.

[6] **Glorification** – The work of God in believers to bring them to the ultimate and perfect stage of salvation—Christlikeness—following his justification and sanctification of them (Rom. 8:29–30). Glorification includes believers' receiving imperishable resurrection bodies at Christ's return (1 Cor. 15:42–43).

WEEK 9: THE LAST BATTLE

Ezekiel 38:1–39:29

▲

The Place of the Passage

Although this is one of the most enigmatic passages in all of Scripture, the basic point of these chapters is clear. Having promised to restore his people and dwell in their midst (Ezekiel 34–37), God now declares that in the latter days he will bring against Israel a mighty foe, allied with all the nations, and then will utterly defeat that foe. God will thus display "my greatness and my holiness . . . in the eyes of many nations" (38:23). This defeat will be so complete and final that Israel will never again doubt that the Lord is God (39:22).

The Big Picture

God will not only restore his people but will also vindicate his reputation by delivering them from every enemy forever.

> ## Reflection and Discussion

Read through the complete passage for this study, Ezekiel 38–39. Then review the questions below concerning this section of Ezekiel and write your notes on them. (For further background, see the *ESV Study Bible*, pages 1560–1563; available online at esv.org.)

1. The Defeat of Gog (38:1–23)

The precise identity of Gog of Magog (38:2) is unknown. Some have suggested a future ruler from Asia Minor, which is to the north of Israel, or from even further afield. At one level, it is possible that this is even a reference to Babylon, the only contemporary neighbor of Israel not judged in chapters 25–32. But other details suggest that Gog is a symbolic figure, representing all of the forces of evil intent on destroying God's people. This is how John appears to use this passage in Revelation 20:7–10. What descriptions in 38:1–23 suggest a symbolic interpretation? What does "the latter years/days" (38:8, 16) refer to?

Why does Gog seek to pursue this war against God's people (38:10–13)? Who is the ultimate author of Gog's plans (38:4, 16)? How does this help us to understand the relationship between human plans and designs and God's sovereignty?

How does God respond to Gog's attack on his people (38:18–22)? The imagery of God's war-like wrath is drawn from the plagues against Egypt (see Exodus 7–10; Psalm 18) and is picked up by John in Revelation 16:18–21. What does this suggest about the nature of this battle and the deliverance God brings to his people?

Why does God precipitate this climactic battle (Ezek. 38:23)? What does this teach us about God and his plans?

2. The Sacrifice of Gog (39:1–24)

Chapter 39 reiterates the message of the previous chapter and develops it. How does 39:1–8 further develop and apply the idea that God is in total control of Gog's war against Israel? Why do these events reveal God to be the "Holy One in Israel" (39:7)?

Three different images are used to describe the final fate of Gog and his armies. They are plundered (39:9–10), buried (vv. 11–16), and devoured as a sacrificial feast (vv. 17–20). How does each image contribute to the sense of the finality of this battle? Is there irony, or poetic justice, at work in these images? If so, how? What is particularly ironic about the sacrificial feast imagery? Why would God invert this image? (see Isa. 34:1–10; Zeph. 1:7–9).

There are seven nations included in Gog's alliance (Ezek. 38:2–6). Seven kinds of plunder are listed in Gog's defeat, and they are burned for seven years (39:9). It takes seven months to bury the dead and cleanse the land (39:12). Seven judgments are listed in 38:21–22, and there are seven items on the menu in 39:18. The two chapters together are composed of seven oracles introduced by the phrase, "Thus says the Lord GOD." What is being communicated by this repeated use of the number seven? What encouragement are we to take from these grisly scenes?

Once again, what is God's purpose in this judgment, first for the nations and then for Israel (39:21–22)? Why does God want the nations to know that Israel has already been punished for her iniquity through her captivity and exile (39:23–24)?

3. God's Purpose for Israel (39:25–29)

The passage concludes with a promise of restoration to the land. Given the context, when should we expect this promise to be fulfilled, and whom will it include? How does 39:29 tie this promise back into earlier promises in Ezekiel (see 36:27 and 37:1–14)?

What does it say about the Lord's deliverance that, afterward, Israel will "forget their shame and all the treachery they have practiced against me"? How does our salvation "vindicate" God's "holiness in the sight of many nations" (39:26–27)?

Read through the following three sections on *Gospel Glimpses*, *Whole-Bible Connections*, and *Theological Soundings*. Then take time to consider the *Personal Implications* these sections may have for you.

Gospel Glimpses

THE CROSS OF CHRIST GUARANTEES THE JUDGMENT OF SIN. In Ezekiel 39:23, the defeat of Gog assures the nations that Israel's captivity was not because of God's weakness but because of his justice. God could have prevented the captivity of his people, but instead he ordained it for his purposes of judging and refining his people. In the same way, Jesus Christ's death on the cross was a sign not of God's inability to save his Son but of his commitment to judge and punish sin. The cross of Christ is a demonstration of God's commitment to judge all sin, either in Christ at the cross (for all those who turn to him in faith) or by the crucified and risen Christ at the end of the ages (for all who refuse in this life to place their hope in him).

Whole-Bible Connections

GOG AND MAGOG. In Genesis 10:2, Magog is identified as one of the sons of Japheth. Thus Ezekiel has rooted his prophecy in ancient history. But his image of a terrifying prince of darkness opposed to God's people points to the future as well. In Revelation 20:7–10, Gog is inspired and led by Satan, and their attack is not against ethnic Israel but against the "camp of the saints and the beloved city." Jesus now occupies the throne of David, and Satan's battle is against all who bend their knee to Christ. But, as in the battle that Ezekiel envisions (38:22), in Revelation fire comes down from heaven, and God himself fights for and delivers his people. Until the last day, God's people will know oppression and peril in this world. In the meantime, however, we may take heart, for Jesus has "overcome the world" (John 16:33).

Theological Soundings

ESCHATOLOGY. Eschatology is the study of the "last things" and pertains to what God has revealed about the course and end of history. With the death and resurrection of Jesus Christ, the "last days" have begun, according to the New Testament authors (see Acts 2:17; Heb. 1:2). Sometimes the Bible uses apocalyptic[1] imagery and language to teach about the last things. The point in doing so is not to confuse or obscure but rather to encourage God's people, as Ezekiel did. We may not understand all of the details, but we know that God is the Lord of history and is bringing all things to the conclusion that he has designed: the salvation of his people and the exaltation of his Son, Jesus Christ.

Personal Implications

Take time to reflect on the implications of Ezekiel 38–39 for your own life today. Consider what you have learned that might lead you to praise God, repent of sin, and trust more deeply in his gracious promises. Write down your reflections under the three headings we have considered and on the passage as a whole.

1. Gospel Glimpses

2. Whole-Bible Connections

3. Theological Soundings

----

4. Ezekiel 38–39

As You Finish This Unit . . .

Take a moment now to ask for the Lord's blessing and help as you continue in this study of Ezekiel. And take a moment also to look back through this unit of study, to reflect on some key things that the Lord may be teaching you.

Definition

[1] **Apocalyptic** – The distinctive literary form of the book of Revelation and of chapters 7–12 of Daniel. These parts of Scripture include revelation about the future, highly symbolic imagery, and the underlying belief that God himself will one day end the world in its present form and establish his kingdom on earth.

Week 10: The New Temple

Ezekiel 40:1–46:24

The Place of the Passage

With the final defeat of both human and spiritual evil (Ezekiel 38–39), the way is paved for God to dwell with his people. Chapter 40 introduces the beginning of the end of the book, and these chapters relate the final vision Ezekiel receives. In contrast to the abominations[1] Ezekiel saw in chapters 8–11, he now sees a new temple. After a tour of its rooms (chs. 40–42), Ezekiel witnesses the glory of the Lord returning to fill his temple (43:1–12). As the tour resumes (43:13–46:24), Ezekiel is given instructions for Israel's renewed worship. Through this vision God makes clear that he will never again leave his people, and they will never again leave him.

The Big Picture

Despite their sin, God will be with his people forever.

> ## Reflection and Discussion

Read through the complete passage for this study, Ezekiel 40–46. Then review the questions below concerning this section of Ezekiel and write your notes on them. (For further background, see the *ESV Study Bible*, pages 1564–1576; available online at esv.org.)

1. A New Temple (40:1–42:20)

How does Ezekiel let us know that we should read this vision against the contrast of chapters 8–11 (40:1–4)? Why is Ezekiel given this vision?

The details of the new temple are not necessarily riveting for the modern reader, but the temple was the primary symbol of Israel's identity. Given what the exiles have been through, and especially the news of the destruction of the temple in Jerusalem, what is the purpose of these details? Why does Ezekiel's tour begin and end at the east gate (see 10:19; 11:23)? Why is the climax of the tour not the Most Holy Place (41:4)?

While many architectural and ornamental details are provided, much of the temple is left without description. As with the vision of God's chariot-throne in chapter 1, Ezekiel is given not a blueprint but rather "visions of God" (40:2). The final measurements, 500 cubits square, are ideal and perfect (42:15–20).

In light of this, who is the implied builder of this temple, and what does the temple reveal about that builder?

----

2. The Glory of God Returns (43:1–12)

In 43:1, God returns from the same direction in which he had left. Having earlier witnessed his departure, Ezekiel now beholds how "the glory of the LORD entered the temple" (43:4). Why is it important for Ezekiel to witness God's glory within the inner rooms? Is this the climax of the book? Explain.

Ezekiel explicitly links his vision of the glory of the Lord to his visions in both chapter 1 and chapters 8–11. Why is this important? How else does God assure his people that he has returned and will not leave them again (43:7–9)?

God says that "*if* they are ashamed of all that they have done," *then* Ezekiel is to "make known" these temple plans to the people, because the entire temple mount is to be "most holy" (43:11–12). What is being hinted at by the fact that the entire temple mount, and not just the inner sanctuary, is "most holy?" How do humility and repentance allow God's people to be in his presence?

---

3. A Renewed People (43:13–46:24)

The next section of the vision focuses less on the temple structure itself and more on what takes place there. Ezekiel is given instruction for the renewed worship of God's people. The last time God's people were given such detailed instructions was in the wilderness as they prepared to enter the Promised Land (see Exodus 29; Leviticus 8). What does this fact say about Ezekiel's role in this passage? What does it suggest about the context for the fulfillment of this vision in the future?

According to 43:26–27, what are the purpose and the result of Israel's renewed worship? How does this statement answer the driving question of Ezekiel and the exiles?

In 44:1–14, various instructions are provided about the gates of the temple. The east gate of the sanctuary is shut and is never to be opened again (44:1–3). Why? What does this imply about God's presence going forward? Who is excluded from the temple, and who is included (44:4–9)? Why are the unfaithful Levites singled out for restricted service (44:10–14)?

In chapters 44–46, special instructions are given for the "prince." Who is this figure (see 34:24; 37:25)? What special privileges and duties are accorded to this prince in worship (see 44:3; 45:13–25; 46:1–12)? What is the significance of the fact that the prince provides the sacrifice for the sin of the people (45:16–17)?

At the regular feasts, all of the people are to come before the Lord, entering from the north and exiting in the south, or vice versa. And though the prince stands in the east gate, he enters and leaves with the people (46:9–12). What does this say about the prince and his relation to both God and the people? What does their movement, which requires them to pass by the east gate, communicate (see 43:7)?

Read through the following three sections on *Gospel Glimpses*, *Whole-Bible Connections*, and *Theological Soundings*. Then take time to consider the *Personal Implications* these sections may have for you.

Gospel Glimpses

THE PRINCE OF PEACE. Throughout Ezekiel, God has promised a prince from the line of David to rule over his people in righteousness. But when that prince appears in the final temple vision, he not only rules, he also provides the sacrifice for sin and the Passover sacrifice that the people need (45:16–17, 21–25). God would ultimately accomplish his desire to dwell with us by providing us a Prince of Peace who would provide the sacrifice that his people need in order to be clean. That prince is Jesus, and the sacrifice he offered was none other than himself. Through his selfless death and powerful resurrection, Jesus proved himself to be an effective atoning sacrifice for the sins of his people, and the great Prince who has defeated all of his people's enemies, even death.

Whole-Bible Connections

MEASURING THE TEMPLE. The precise measurements of Ezekiel's temple echo the precise measurements of the earlier temple constructed by Solomon, although the measurements for Ezekiel's temple are much larger and grander (compare 1 Kings 6). But the point of the measurements is the same whenever they appear: God's dwelling with his people is according to his specifications, and it is perfect; nothing is missing or out of place. But when this vision of measuring is taken up in Revelation 21:15ff., a passage that clearly alludes to and references this passage in Ezekiel in many ways, it is not the temple that is being measured but the entire heavenly city. Why is no temple measured? The answer is that John "saw no temple in the city, for its temple is the Lord God the Almighty and the Lamb" (Rev. 21:22). When the Lord fills the new heavens and the new earth, there will be no need for a localized structure to contain his presence.

Theological Soundings

EZEKIEL'S TEMPLE AND MILLENNIAL VIEWS. Ultimately, how we interpret Ezekiel's vision of the temple depends on how we think it will be fulfilled. We know that it was not fulfilled entirely in past history, for those who remembered Solomon's temple wept when they saw the foundation of Ezra's temple (Ezra 3:12), which was built after the time of Ezekiel, when the people of God were allowed to return to the land of Israel. Some believe that Ezekiel's temple will be built as part of a literal millennial kingdom of Christ on earth, with sacrifices that commemorate his perfect sacrifice. Others believe that Ezekiel's temple is symbolic of God's presence among his people in the church and their renewed worship in Christ (see 1 Pet. 2:5). Consistent with, but not identical to, the second view is the belief that this vision points forward to the same reality of which Revelation 21 speaks: the eternal worship of God's people in the new creation. While serious believers hold various views, all can agree that Ezekiel's vision promises that God will once again dwell with his people, and that he will accomplish that in and through Jesus Christ, the true temple of God (Rev. 21:22).

Personal Implications

Take time to reflect on the implications of Ezekiel 40–46 for your own life today. Consider what you have learned that might lead you to praise God, repent of sin, and trust more deeply in his gracious promises. Write down your reflections under the three headings we have considered and on the passage as a whole.

1. Gospel Glimpses

2. Whole-Bible Connections

3. Theological Soundings

4. Ezekiel 40–46

> ### As You Finish This Unit . . .

Take a moment now to ask for the Lord's blessing and help as you continue in this study of Ezekiel. And take a moment also to look back through this unit of study, to reflect on some key things that the Lord may be teaching you.

Definition

[1] **Abomination** – Something that deeply offends. This term often describes something that offends God and his standard of holiness. The Bible also mentions the "abomination of desolation" (or "abomination that makes desolate"), apparently referring to some profane act or object wrongfully permitted in the temple (Dan. 11:31; 12:11; Matt. 24:15).

WEEK 11: THE NEW CREATION

Ezekiel 47:1–48:35

▲

Ezekiel's vision does not end with the temple. In chapter 45, the prophet described the temple district, and now the camera zooms out even further. The city and the land are described, and it is nothing less than a vision of the new creation. In chapter 47, a river flows from the temple, starting small and growing into a rushing river that gives life to the dead land and turns the Dead Sea into a teeming, vibrant lake. The rest of chapters 47–48 describes the boundaries and division of the land. At the center, in the midst of the people, is the city of the Lord, with the new temple in the very center. The vision concludes with the animating promise of the entire book: the name of the city is not Jerusalem but "The LORD Is There."

The Big Picture

God's presence among his people makes all things new.

> ## Reflection and Discussion

Read through the complete passage for this study, Ezekiel 47–48. Then review the questions below concerning this section of Ezekiel and write your notes on them. (For further background, see the *ESV Study Bible*, pages 1576–1580; available online at esv.org.)

1. The Temple's River (47:1–12)

Flowing from the threshold of the sanctuary itself is a stream (47:1–2). What is the significance of its source? Where else has water appeared in Ezekiel in the context of blessing (see 36:24–30)? Are these two appearances related?

What happens to the river as it flows (47:3–6)? What is the significance of its growth (compare Mark 4:30–32)? Why would this be especially important for the exiles to understand?

The sea that the river flows into is the Dead Sea (47:8). What effect does the water have on the sea and its environs (47:7–12)? Why does Ezekiel use the relatively rare verb "swarms" (47:9; compare Gen. 1:20–21)? What is the significance of the trees on either side of the river that bear fruit every month, and whose leaves are for healing (see Gen. 1:29; 2:9; Rev. 22:1–2)? Is Ezekiel merely describing the region of the Dead Sea, or is this a vision of something greater?

2. The Division of the Land (47:13–48:29)

Having described the fruitful and abundant life of the new creation that flows from the temple, Ezekiel is informed of the boundaries and division of the "land for inheritance" that God "swore to give to your fathers" (47:13–14). Are the new boundaries the same as the historical boundaries (47:15–23)? What might it mean if the boundaries *did* match what was originally described in Numbers 34?

As the specific allotments are given to the 12 tribes, what is different from the historical tribal allotments (48:1–29; compare Joshua 15–19)? What suggests that these are idealized boundaries rather than literal ones? What is the point of the allotments being equal? How does this contribute to the idea that Ezekiel is describing the entire new creation rather than merely Palestine?

Where is "the city" in the allotments of the tribes (48:8–22)? Where is the temple in this city (vv. 8, 21)? How is the city allotted (vv. 10–22)? In addition to the priests and Levites, who works in the city (v. 19)? Why is the city un-named? Taken together, what is the significance of these details concerning the city?

3. The City of God (48:30–35)

Having described the allotments for the tribes, Ezekiel ends with one last look at the city. What is described in 48:30–34? What is the significance of gates in general? What is the theological point of the 12 gates?

Gates have been prominent in Ezekiel's two temple visions (chs. 8–11; 40–46). God left by the east gate in 10:19, and he returned by the same gate in 43:2. That gate was shut permanently (44:2). Now the vision ends with a focus on the gates for the people of God. This same image is used in Revelation 21:12–13. In Revelation 21:25, John tells us that the gates of the new city will never be shut. How does this vision give hope and endurance to God's people as they wait for its fulfillment?

What is the name of the city (48:35)? Why is it not called Jerusalem? How does this verse address the central issue of the book of Ezekiel? Why is it a fitting conclusion?

Read through the following three sections on *Gospel Glimpses, Whole-Bible Connections*, and *Theological Soundings*. Then take time to consider the *Personal Implications* these sections may have for you.

Gospel Glimpses

LIVING WATER. In an arid climate like the ancient Near East, water was a constant concern. As the Patriarchs traveled through the land, for example, they dug multiple wells (Gen. 21:25–31; 26:18–25). In a wilderness without wells, Moses was told first to strike a rock (Ex. 17:6), and later to speak to it (Num. 20:8ff.). From this rock flowed water that sustained the life of Israel in their wandering. Now Ezekiel sees life-giving water flowing from the sanctuary itself. But the true water of life was not water at all but rather the triune God. In John 4:1–26, Jesus speaks to a Samaritan woman beside a well, offering her water that would become a "spring of water welling up to eternal life"[1] (John 4:14). Later, he would declare, "Whoever believes in me, as the Scripture has said, 'Out of his heart will flow rivers of living water.' Now this he said about the Spirit" (John 7:38–39). Jesus, the true Rock (1 Cor. 10:4), the son of God, gives the water of life, the Spirit of God, so that all who believe in him might know God the Father, who declares, "To the thirsty, I will give from the spring of the water of life without payment" (Rev. 21:6).

FISHERS OF MEN. In Ezekiel's vision the Dead Sea comes alive, teeming with fish. And on its banks stand fishermen, spreading their nets and catching "fish . . . of very many kinds, like the fish of the Great Sea [the Mediterranean]" (47:10). Jeremiah uses the image of fishers of men in the context of calling Israel back from idolatry (Jer. 16:16), but here the context is clearly one of blessing and abundance. No kind of fish will be lacking. While Jeremiah 16 is clearly in Jesus' mind when he calls his disciples to be "fishers of men" (Matt. 4:19), perhaps he is thinking of Ezekiel 48 as well. Certainly this detail gives us believers confidence in our message. As we go about the work of evangelism, we can be certain that in the end, the new creation will be well and fully populated with fish of every kind, representing "all tribes and peoples and languages" (Rev. 7:9).

Whole-Bible Connections

TREE OF LIFE. At the center of the garden of Eden stood the tree of life (Gen. 2:9). If Adam and Eve had not sinned, they presumably would have retained access to the tree and thus would have been enabled to live forever in a state of blessing. But God specifically banished man from the garden after the fall[2] "lest he reach out his hand and take also of the tree of life and eat, and live forever" (Gen. 3:22). At that point in the biblical story, the tree of life disappears from view, hidden behind the flaming sword of the cherubim. But it is not coincidental that first the tabernacle, and then the temple, were decorated with trees (see 1 Kings 6), reminiscent of the garden of Eden. These decorations were symbolic and pointed to the goal, which had not changed. The tree of life does not reappear by name until Revelation. There we are told that the tree appears on both sides of the river of the water of life flowing down the middle of the city from the throne of God. It bears fruit every month, and its leaves "were for the healing of the nations" (Rev. 22:1–2). Clearly John is familiar with Ezekiel's vision. But what does this tree of life represent? Although it was a literal tree in Eden, it seems to be a figurative tree in the visions of Ezekiel and John. Does this tree not represent Christ, whose cross, that accursed tree, has become a tree of life for all who believe?

CREATION/RE-CREATION. One of the main ways in which Scripture portrays the hope of salvation is through the imagery of re-creation. Ezekiel provides many hints that the new creation, rather than merely Palestine, is in view in these chapters. From the river of life that flows from the temple, to the tree of life lining the river's banks, to the transformation of the Dead Sea into a teeming lake, to the idealized borders and allotments of the land, and finally to the name of the city, Ezekiel is painting a picture that goes beyond the limits of a fallen world and in fact harks back to Eden (see Gen. 2:5–14). Here is the great hope of biblical religion: not that God will merely make this world better, but that he will make the world new; not that God will merely make us better, but that he will make us new. This is not to say there will be no continuity between this world and the next. Some New Testament passages stress discontinuity (2 Pet. 3:7), while others point to continuity (Rom. 8:20–22). But regardless of where that line is drawn, when God brings his work of salvation to completion, all sin, all corruption, all evil, all futility—everything associated with the curse—will be gone. And in its place, God declares, "Behold, I am making all things new" (Rev. 21:5).

> ## Theological Soundings

HOLY SPIRIT. The Holy Spirit is the third person of the Trinity, and his role in the economy of salvation is well illustrated in two of the main images used of him in Ezekiel: breath and water. The Holy Spirit is the one who breathes life into our dead spirits, just as he breathed life into the dead bodies in the valley of dry bones (ch. 37). He is also the one who cleanses us, like water, from our guilty conscience, as he applies the merits of Christ's shed blood to us, making us not merely ceremonially clean but inwardly clean as well (ch. 36). Having made us alive and clean, he sustains our life in Christ and causes us to grow and be fruitful, like a well-watered tree (ch. 47). But the growth is not merely individual. Like that stream here in Ezekiel that became a rushing river that could not be crossed, the Holy Spirit causes the whole church to grow and spread as the kingdom of God expands in all of its glory and God again dwells in his people through his Spirit (Eph. 2:22).

PROMISE-FULFILLMENT. The entire Scripture has a prophetic character, in which God makes promises and then fulfills them. Sometimes those promises are fulfilled in very straightforward ways, as when God promised Sarah she would have a son in her old age (Gen. 18:10), and about a year later Isaac was born (Gen. 21:1–2). But often the promises of God have multiple horizons of fulfillment, as the ultimate fulfillment is far greater than the original recipients conceived; it often even takes unexpected forms. Nowhere is that dynamic more evident than in a passage like Ezekiel 47–48. From the end of the story in Revelation 22:1–5, we know that Ezekiel's vision of a temple with a river flowing from it is finally fulfilled not in Palestine but in the new creation. The ultimate point is not a literal temple or river but the life-giving presence of God with his people in unmediated intimacy. From the middle of the story, we know from John 2, 4, and 7 that Jesus claimed to be that temple, and that he was the source of the true water of life, which is the Spirit. Does this mean that God did not keep his promise to Ezekiel and the exiles, implied in the vision that concludes the book? Not at all. It simply means that the promise was even better than they imagined, and that its fulfillment was greater than they knew, for they "did not receive what was promised, since God had provided something better for us" (Heb. 11:39–40)—and that "something better" is found in Christ.

Personal Implications

Take time to reflect on the implications of Ezekiel 47–48 for your own life today. Consider what you have learned that might lead you to praise God, repent of sin, and trust more deeply in his gracious promises. Write down your reflections under the three headings we have considered and on the passage as a whole.

1. Gospel Glimpses

2. Whole-Bible Connections

3. Theological Soundings

4. Ezekiel 47–48

As You Finish This Unit . . .

Take a moment now to ask for the Lord's blessing and help as you continue in this study of Ezekiel. And take a moment also to look back through this unit of study, to reflect on some key things that the Lord may be teaching you.

Definitions

[1] **Eternal Life** – For believers, the new life that begins with trust in Jesus Christ alone for salvation and that continues after physical death with an eternity in God's presence, with resurrected and glorified bodies in the new heavens and the new earth.

[2] **The fall** – Adam and Eve's disobedience of God by eating the fruit from the tree of the knowledge of good and evil, resulting in their loss of innocence and favor with God and the introduction of sin and its effects into the world (Genesis 2; Rom. 5:12–21; 1 Cor. 15:21–22).

WEEK 12: SUMMARY AND CONCLUSION

▲

We conclude our study of Ezekiel by summarizing the big picture of God's message through the book as a whole. Then we will consider several questions in order to reflect on various Gospel Glimpses, Whole-Bible Connections, and Theological Soundings throughout the entire book.

The Big Picture of Ezekiel

While enigmatic to many and shocking to most, we have seen that the book of Ezekiel has not only a clear structure but also a compelling message, both to his original audience in exile and to God's people today, who are "elect exiles" in this world (1 Pet. 1:1).

Ezekiel is captured by a vision of the glory of God (chs. 1–3). And with that vision controlling him, he confronts people who have to face the unthinkable—the loss of their identity and seeming abandonment by God—but are unwilling to do so (chs. 4–24). Again and again, through visions, prophecy, parable, and even street theater, Ezekiel calls God's people to face up to the truth of the bad news. Their sinful treachery against God by taking idols into their hearts and forsaking God's covenant has finally brought upon them the judgment that such rebellion deserves. While, politically, they are caught up in the tangled international affairs of competing empires, ultimately the army of Babylon is merely the sword in God's hand, executing his covenant curses. No amount of protestations of innocence or injustice, no appeals to history or heritage, can change that outcome. God has withdrawn his glory from the temple and his people, and they have no one to blame but themselves.

It takes time for news of the fall of Jerusalem to reach the exiles in Babylon. As the fugitive bearing the news makes his way, the narrative camera, as it were, pans out over the surrounding nations (chs. 25–32). It would be easy to conclude that in Jerusalem's defeat, the gods of Babylon have vanquished the God of Israel. But these chapters paint a different story. God has disciplined his people, but now he will turn and defeat their enemies, near and far, small and great. God fights for his people, and not just against their political enemies. Ultimately, God will defeat the prince of evil himself, the Satanic figure animating all opposition to God's people (28:1–19).

When news of Jerusalem's fall finally reaches the exiles (ch. 33), Ezekiel's message turns to visions of hope and restoration (chs. 34–48). Having been betrayed and failed by their leaders, they hear God declare that he will be their Shepherd and will provide a messianic Shepherd-King. And he will not simply renew the old covenant, offering them a second chance. He will make a new covenant of peace with his people and will actually change them from the inside out by his Spirit so that they can keep the covenant he makes with them. Though to all appearances they are a dead nation, God will make them alive. And the day will come when he will finally and forever defeat their greatest enemy and reestablish his presence in their midst in a new temple with renewed worship in the new creation itself.

Through both judgment and salvation, God is committed to vindicating his glory and the holiness of his name. And so his call to repentance and faith throughout Ezekiel is matched by his gift of the Spirit and the new life that makes such faith possible. In the context of the bitter defeat of exile and the despairing question, "Where is God?," Ezekiel provides the answer: God is with his people, a sanctuary for them in exile in the present age, the source of life in the midst of death, and, in the age to come, the temple in which God will dwell with his people forever.

Read through the following three sections on *Gospel Glimpses*, *Whole-Bible Connections*, and *Theological Soundings*. Then take time to consider the *Personal Implications* these sections may have for you.

Gospel Glimpses

Throughout our study we have seen that Ezekiel points to and prepares us for the gospel of Jesus Christ. First, he is unrelenting in his indictment of idolatry and the judgment such spiritual treachery deserves. This is the bad news of the gospel. But second, he also points us to the good news of hope for restoration and renewed intimacy with God. Three images stand out in this regard. First, the exiles despair in the loss of the temple, but their hope is renewed through the promise of a new temple that God will never leave. In the New Testament, we learn that Jesus is that temple (John 2). As the God-man, he is literally the place where God and man meet, and through his priestly ministry of sacrifice and intercession he brings us into the presence of God. What is more, he is building us into a temple of God as well.

Second, Israel's exile is precipitated politically by a colossal failure of leadership by her kings and spiritually by both priests and kings who lead the people into idolatry. In response, God promises not only to be their Shepherd but also to provide a Shepherd-King who will sit on David's throne and lead his people to good pastures. Not only will that messianic King lead, he will also provide the sacrifice for his people's sin in the new temple. All of these promises will be fulfilled in Jesus, descended from David, as the Good Shepherd (John 10) who lays down his life as a sacrifice for his sheep.

Finally, in response to the broken covenant that precipitates God's curses, the Lord promises to establish a new covenant of peace, in which he will not only cleanse his people but will also put his Spirit within them, giving them new hearts and spiritual life so that they might keep his covenant. Jesus comes offering the water of life that cleanses and makes alive, the Holy Spirit himself (John 3–4), and he establishes this new covenant through his blood, proving it through the outpouring of the Spirit at Pentecost after his resurrection and ascension.[1]

Has Ezekiel brought new clarity to your understanding of the gospel? How so?

Were there any particular passages or themes in Ezekiel that led you to have a fresh understanding and grasp of God's grace to us through Jesus?

Whole-Bible Connections

Ezekiel's vision centers on the glory of God and the question of how God can dwell with his people. The controlling image, therefore, is the temple, the physical and symbolic location of the presence of God in his glory in the midst of his people. As Ezekiel explores God's departure from the temple in Jerusalem and his eventual return to the visionary temple of chapters 40–48, Ezekiel draws repeatedly on language descriptive of both the garden of Eden and the Promised Land in order to paint a picture of God's dwelling with his people in the new creation. As a result, Ezekiel connects the history of Israel to the overarching storyline of the Bible: creation, fall/exile, restoration, and consummation.[2] Israel's exile is a recapitulation of Adam's fall, and Israel's hope is a new covenant accomplished by God himself. Through a messianic Shepherd-King, God's people obtain not merely forgiveness but also cleansing and regeneration by the Spirit of God so that once again God can dwell with his people. While never losing sight of the immediate context of the exiles, Ezekiel paints a picture that comprehends the entire scope of redemptive history.[3]

How has this study of Ezekiel filled out your understanding of the biblical storyline of redemption?

Are any themes emphasized in Ezekiel that help to deepen your grasp of the Bible's unity?

Have any passages or themes expanded your understanding of the redemption that Jesus provides, begun at his first coming and consummated at his return?

What connections between Ezekiel and the New Testament were new to you? What would you like to explore further?

_____

_____

_____

_____

Theological Soundings

Ezekiel has much to contribute to Christian theology. Numerous doctrines and themes are developed, clarified, and reinforced throughout, such as the glory of God, the presence of God, the work of the Holy Spirit, the sovereignty of God in salvation, idolatry as adultery, the holiness of God, and the motivations of God in both judgment and salvation.

Has your theology shifted or developed in large or small ways during the course of studying Ezekiel? How so?

_____

_____

_____

_____

How has your understanding of the nature and character of God been deepened throughout this study?

_____

_____

_____

_____

What unique contributions does Ezekiel make toward our understanding of who Jesus is and what he accomplished through his life, death, and resurrection?

_____

_____

_____

_____

_____

What specifically does Ezekiel teach us about the human condition and our need of redemption?

Personal Implications

God gave us the book of Ezekiel to convict us of sin and to give us hope in his commitment to save his people through his Son for the sake of his glory. If our study of this book does not lead us to a clearer vision of God's glory in the gospel and thus to more faithful worship, we have been wasting our time. As you reflect on Ezekiel as a whole, what implications do you see for your life?

What life implications flow from your reflections on the questions already asked in this week's study concerning Gospel Glimpses, Whole-Bible Connections, and Theological Soundings?

What has this book brought home to you that leads you to praise God, turn away from sin, and trust more firmly in his promises?

How has your hope in God's promise to be with you been renewed or strengthened?

As You Finish Studying Ezekiel . . .

We rejoice with you as you finish studying the book of Ezekiel! May this study become part of your Christian walk of faith, day by day and week by week throughout all your life. Now we would greatly encourage you to study the Word of God in an ongoing way. To help you as you continue your study of the Bible, we would encourage you to consider other books in the *Knowing the Bible* series, and to visit knowingthebibleseries.org.

Lastly, take a moment to look back through this study. Review the notes that you have written, and the things that you have highlighted or underlined. Reflect again on the key themes that the Lord has been teaching you about himself and about his Word. May these things become a treasure for you throughout your life—which we pray in the name of the Father, and the Son, and the Holy Spirit. Amen.

Definitions

[1] **Ascension** – The departure of the resurrected Jesus to God the Father in heaven (Luke 24:50–51; Acts 1:1–11).

[2] **Consummation** – In Christian theology, the final and full establishment of the kingdom of God, when the heavens and earth will be made new and God will rule over all things forever (2 Pet. 3:13; Revelation 11; 19–22).

[3] **Redemptive history/history of salvation** – God's unified plan for all of history to accomplish the salvation of his people. He accomplished this salvation plan in the work of Jesus Christ on earth, by his life, crucifixion, burial, and resurrection (Eph. 1:3–23). The consummation of God's plan will take place when Jesus Christ comes again to establish the "new heavens and a new earth in which righteousness dwells" (2 Pet. 3:13).

KNOWING THE BIBLE STUDY GUIDE SERIES

Experience the *Grace* of God in the *Word* of God, Book by Book

────────────── **Series Volumes** ──────────────

crossway.org/knowingthebible